Having a Little Talk
with Capital P Poetry

BOOKS BY JIM DANIELS

Poetry:

Factory Poems
On the Line
Places/Everyone
The Long Ball
Digger's Territory
Punching Out
Hacking It
M-80
Niagara Falls
Blessing the House
Blue Jesus
Red Vinyl, Black Vinyl
Night with Drive-By Shooting Stars
Greatest Hits
Digger's Blues
Show and Tell: New and Selected Poems
Street (with photographs by Charlee Brodsky)
Now Showing
Revolt of the Crash-Test Dummies
In Line for the Exterminator

Fiction:

No Pets
Detroit Tales
Mr. Pleasant

Having a Little Talk with Capital P Poetry

Poems by Jim Daniels

Carnegie Mellon University Press
Pittsburgh 2010

ACKNOWLEDGMENTS

5 a.m.: "Tenured Guy and the Chalk-Throwing Incident"

The Antioch Review: "Don Ho Esperanto"

Breathe: 101 Contemporary Odes, Eds. Chad Prevost, Ryan Van Cleave: "Ode to the Reel Mower"

Cerise Press: "Complete Lack of Home Movies," "Hammering"

Chautauqua: "Ella Fitzgerald Esperanto," "Miles Davis Esperanto," "Bonnie Raitt Esperanto," "Reincarnation of the Peace Sign"

The Connecticut Review: "Having a Little Talk with Capital P Poetry," "Dogs Do It"

Drunken Boat: "Sex Pistols Esperanto," "Duane Allman Esperanto," "Al Green Esperanto," "James Brown Esperanto"

Dunes Review: "Landscape with Gum Wrapper"

Eclipse: "The Tenured Guy Examines His Conscience"

Exquisite Corpse: "Tenured Guy Learns to Cook," "Tenured Guy and Artistic Standards," "Tenured Guy on Sabbatical," "Tenured Guy Calculates Salaries"

Field: "Judy Garland Esperanto," "Joe Cocker Esperanto," "David Bowie Esperanto"

Folio: "Bag of Clothes"

The Fourth River: "Landfill America," "Defeat in the City Game"

Gargoyle: "The Abyssinian Baptist Gospel Choir Esperanto," "Marvin Gaye Esperanto"

Georgetown Review: "Dream with a Train in It"

Gigantic Sequins: "Tarnish"

Grand Valley Review: "The Tenured Guy and the Chalk-Throwing Incident"

Green Mountains Review: "I Lost My Voice in a Mall"

Gulf Stream: "The Name of the Place"

The Iron Horse Literary Review: "For the Young Boy Who Cheered the Nazis During the 'Sing-a-Long Sound of Music'"

Lake Effect: "Indecipherable Elegy"

Midwest Quarterly Review: "Winter Notion"

The Nebraska Review: "The Wrist"

The Paterson Literary Review: "Last Picked," "The Garden State," "March 20, 2003"

Pearl: "Tenured Guy: Department Meeting, Friday Afternoon"

Pembroke: "Biting Off More"

Poetry East: "Walking My Son Home from Preschool"

poetrymagazine.com: "Wildflowers Dying in a Cracked Vase"

Quixote Quarterly: "The Tenured Guy Goes into Orbit"

Rockhurst Review: "Attendance Police"

Riverwind: "The Tenured Guy Reads His Student Evaluations"

Slant: "The Tenured Guy Handles the Evidence"

The South Carolina Review: "Hammering" (as "Tightening the Vise")

The Southern Review: "Aerial View, Warren, Michigan," "Rusty Jackknife"
Superstition Review: "Hole in the Theory"
Tampa Review: "Dusty Springfield Esperanto"
The Third Coast: "Last Night A Reckless Cyclist"
Two Review: "Frank Sinatra Esperanto," "Bobby Blue Bland Esperanto," "The Band Esperanto," "Tom Waits Esperanto"

Book design by Drew Johnson

Library of Congress Control Number 2010928354
ISBN 978-0-88748-531-2
Copyright © 2011 by Jim Daniels
Printed and bound in the United States of America

10   9   8   7   6   5   4   3   2   1

CONTENTS

THE TENURED GUY

DEFEAT IN THE CITY GAME

HOLE IN THE THEORY

THE COMPLETE LACK OF HOME MOVIES

from my childhood has allowed our stories
to deteriorate into alternate versions
like some newfangled computer game.
We can change the background from sepia

to neon, to the somber suffocating purple
of the old church. We smudge bordered photos,
clutching black and white against color's
complete disappearance, sunburn and blush

and goddamn pure happiness fading into
the blurry haze of bad color tv, all tint,
no contrast. Ah, memory flickers, film breaking
from endless splices of the heart.

In the dark room unlit by nostalgia's fuse,
our sock puppets turn on us.

Hole in the Theory

I slipped my feet into bread bags,
then rubber boots, a theory
based on faith and poverty.

Clouds in the shape of old friends dissipate
under the scrutiny of unhappy bankers
or maybe just the sun.

I voted this morning. I shook out the floor mats
and vacuumed the car with my dust buster.
The company of losers manufactures

bitterness in small waterproof containers.
I am in touch and out of touch. In reach
and out of reach. Holy water turned to slush.

Holes in that theory, and my feet got soaked.
Damp stench oozed from the back
of the classroom where we hung wet clothes

then took our seats to learn about the simplicity
of God. Memorization's trick, to imagine
permanence. If I stood outside

the polling place and sung the names
of my childhood friends, would anyone
come out to play? A rhetorical theoretical

hypothetical defeat. I bathe in redundancy.
Chance of rain followed by a chance
of more rain. A nun threw away my plastic bags

as if I was cheating. She pointed out the holes
in my logic, and I pointed out the holes in hers.
The cheap buckles broke off one by one.

Jesus emerged from the tomb,
that happy-go-lucky dude. Didn't his
shit stink, I wanted to know.

Just another election-year stunt.
Vote for me and I'll . . .
The perfect hair of politicians is unaffected.

Happy-go-ducky. Happy-stay-nutty.
It was the principle of the thing
that got me expelled.

Behind the toll booth curtain, I confessed
my skepticism and sins and paid my penance
with counterfeit coins. The sun went

hiding, and my old friends returned
nearly unrecognizably Republican.
I loved those boots, wearing them

on the wrong feet for stupid luck.
They made me feel like a lucky duck.
The water gathering in my boots

is the rest of my life.

Aerial View of Warren, Michigan

We played Monopoly in our dark, damp,
unfinished basements, lining up tiny green houses
like gods or general contractors.

Like those houses, ours were identical.
Our favorite songs repeated endless nonsense
syllables. We couldn't get enough sameness,
walking blindfolded into each other's bathrooms

because—because we knew! Rolling the dice—
badoom badoom badoom. Hard splash
onto the square board. We hoarded get-out-of-jail
free cards. We fought over who'd be banker.

We cheated with careful abandon. We purchased
hotels reluctantly, the big red loneliness on all
that space, no open-windowed neighbors screaming.

We stood on stoops and called each other out to play.
We did not trust doorbells or any closed door,
anyone with a piano or a dog of recognizable breed.

Four boys hunched at the board in dusty light,
a whiff of mold, the reckless chirping of a cricket.
Our fathers who art at the factory. No getting lost.
No shortcuts, no twisting paths, no maze of greencry.

Once we cut windows and doors in a refrigerator box.
We rolled it back and forth against the fence.
We bounced our loose limbs off each other.
A mobile home! We joyfully tore it up.

We loved rolling doubles. The dotted lines
of two sixes. We did not understand the concept
of Free Parking or Luxury Tax. Or even Monopoly!

$200 each time we rounded the block?
It just made us dizzy. We had a lot to learn,
but no way were we going to summer school.
We were living it up in Marvin's Gardens!

We constructed basement boxing rings
and smacked each other till we finally
got mad. Whatever adults existed upstairs
pretended they didn't hear.

I know I have stretched the truth about the streets
of Warren, Michigan. Like if I told you Larry Warren
glued all the Monopoly houses down

so we couldn't get them unstuck without ripping
up the board. You can only stretch the truth so far
till it snaps like the rubber band around Chance cards.

If you're passing over in a helicopter or small plane
out of perversity or emergency, you could look
down and see the tiny people emerging
from the tiny houses to wave or give you the finger

or both. We would expect an equally appropriate gesture,
all of us down here—the Iron, the Shoe, the Dog and Wheelbarrow.
Even that weird dude, the Top Hat, a rabbit in each hand,
alone on the corner where we ditched him.

I Lost My Voice in a Mall

The Cadillac dealership sports a white baby grand
in the showroom window, a mirage of desire.
No use dusting for fingerprints.

Wipe that smirk off your face.
Do you want a Smirk, or a Smirk lite?

Listen closely—the batteries are winding
down on the situation comedy clowns.
Their dazed grins suggest they expected more.

Look at the faces on your bills
and say something small and personal.

I'm just one more complaining yo-yo.
Put me to sleep. Here's a short bedtime story:

Once upon a time
every hamburger had a different shape
like snowflakes.

Dogs Do It

They wash each other's
underwear. They solve disputes
with long thoughtful coin
flips. They hold no grudges
or blood-stained sheets.
They think symmetry was invented
by a mad scientist with a messiah complex.
They circle the block with endless expectation
and a complete lack of memory.
They bury things.
They write each other
liquid love notes.
They pluck acoustic guitars.
They answer the phone
when they feel like it.
They make due. They gnaw
on bones and tender mercies.
They get stuck. They get unstuck.
They slurp water like nobody's business.
They shake their whole bodies when wet
in a glorious dance we who have lost our fur
are unable to replicate.
Their only form of prayer
is to roll over in dead things.
They translate everything
into dog, a language with no words.
They let us watch their dreams.

For the Boy Who Cheered the Nazis During the "Sing-a-Long Sound of Music"

The stand-up comic who judged
the costumes told us to hiss
at the Baroness and boo the Nazis.
No Nazis in costume, though countless nuns
roamed the aisles, improvising dramatic blessings.
In our hands, we clutched plastic edelweiss
and a swatch of curtain fabric to wave
at appropriate moments. In the third row
I sat with my wife and kids, lusting after
a young Julie Andrews. Nipples poked against
the fabric of her dress. You'd miss that at home.

Behind us, a family of five—two teenagers
in buzz cuts and football jerseys,
two large women with large hair,
and somebody's sad, quiet daughter.
One of the boys had never seen the movie
and would have preferred watching
the Steelers' game taking place five blocks away.
He missed one of the jokes—*was it about sex?*
he asked. My family obediently hissed and booed.
We *awwwe*d at cute little Gretel.

America gets off on paying for being told
what to do. Okay, I didn't shout *that*
at the screen as a clever comeback.
Americans like shouting out anonymously
in the dark. We waved our edelweiss
at the screen. Julie Andrews bared her breasts
in *Victor, Victoria*—I should rent that again.

I'm channeling the thoughts of a teenager,
number 44, macho mesh jersey cropped.
He said *I want my money back*
when Maria married Captain Von Trapp,
thinking the movie was over. But then
the Nazis showed up. We were all booing
so he thought it'd be funny to cheer.
You don't cheer Nazis, even his brother
knew that: *shut up!*

He'd probably seen *Hogan's Heroes*
reruns on Nickelodeon. I'm waiting for
the Ayatollah and Sadam and Osama shows.
We like to address bad guys by their first names.
Boo the Nazis! Boo Sadam! Hiss the Baroness!
Hiss Osama! Cheer louder on the Noise-o-Meter!

Wave that flag more aggressively. America loves
the epileptic flag waver. Just don't interview him.
Just don't ask him about Jews or Blacks.
He lives in a quaint rural hamlet. He studied
Hamlet in high school and hated it.
He's got a grudge he can't scratch.

I was an idiot waving plastic objects
at a movie screen. I wanted my money back.
Captain Von Trapp ripped the Nazi flag
in half. I know I shouldn't dwell on this
but he treats his kids like Hitler youth
until he meets Maria/Julie.

We're supposed to bark like a dog
whenever Rolf appears. He goes from good
to bad, but he's just a boy, as the Captain says.
The kid behind me, he's just a boy
but he cheered the Nazis. At the end,
he still wanted his money back, even though
it wasn't his money. The five of them
disappeared, back into whatever rural hamlet
from which they emerged. Nobody in their group
sang along.

The nuns traipsed out, a little embarrassed
in the light. The human goatherd puppet
and her puppet master abandoned all pretense
and stood side by side, unwilling to step out
into the sunshine of Sunday afternoon.

Will the boy cheer the Nazis at home?
They lose in every movie but win
small victories daily. Number 44 has left
the building. Toss your edelweiss in the trash.
Squint at the light and try to imagine
saying one clever thing. All I've got
is a shrug and grimace. The bad guys
have a chance out here. My children
don't believe in Little Gretel. All I can say is
Awwwwww. It sounds a bit like *rolf*.

I have made a few generalizations
about America. Easy to do in the dark.
Easy to do what the funny man
tells us to do. Later, we can deny it.
The good team won. The mountains
were beautiful. I lusted after Julie Andrews.
I paid someone money to tell me
to bark like a dog.

Landscape with Gum Wrapper

On the site of the Homestead Steel Mill
stands—sits? squats?—the Waterfront Mall.

The Multi-Mega-Hyper Plex has stadium seating
and fat leather chairs for a fee.

The Monongahela River has fish in it again.
Big ugly fish nobody eats. Nothing

in the Waterfront faces the water. The enormous
parking lot Sunday morning, a frozen lake

of blacktop laced with yellow stripes.
Lined paper to be filled in with the vocabulary
of cars. Direct and indirect objects.

I dreamed I stopped taking my medication
then woke up in the cold-sweat panic

I take the pills for in the first place—I paddle
those long pink canoes through my choppy days.

What floats your boat? I've never seen a canoe
on the Monongahela. Just coal barges I once imagined
as Confessional Boats hauling away sin.

The Waterfront features the Seafood Grille.
You can get fish there. Grilled with an extra E.
Flown in fresh from fish farms.

I love the scrambled letters of the breeze
off the Monongahela—antifreeze and idle rage.

Even Sunday morning, the mill cooked steel.
They make the pills smaller these days.

Shirts on sale at the Target on the Waterfront.
God bless the hammer in the distance
or maybe somebody's knocking endlessly

on the door of abandonment. An enormous man
with bags of stale bread heads down to the river
slumped over as if we were paying him.

ODE TO THE REEL MOWER

When you stop pushing
it stops exactly *there*
absorbing the grace
of cut-grass silence.

*

It always starts. It never runs
out of gas. It does not
shoot your eye out
with a rock or glass shard.

*

It runs on dew and pollen
and sweat. It has never
woken one sleeping person.
It is never new and improved.

*

Grass falls gentle
onto itself like pages
of a favorite book.

*

If the blades need sharpening
a 150-year-old man with a large stone
in a damp basement will send up
faint sparks, accept no payment.

*

At night it trims
the moon's beard.

Landfill America

Off to the landfill with a load of rotten wood
pried from my porch. Stuck in my minivan
between two reeking mammoth garbage trucks,
I climb half-washed-out switchbacks high and higher
into summer drizzle. Lights on, wipers slashing, radio
playing only songs with the word "babe" in them.
I'm driving on packed trash. Beneath me,

who knows what's happening? Not the guy at the gate
with the twisted scar who tells me to unload into his pickup.
He'll take it up later—my van might slide off into the big pit.
Next time just slip your garbage man a twenty
to take this little shit.

I peek over into the abyss of Waste Management Co.
in Monroeville, PA: miles of mad rubble. *Managed*
as in *dumped in a hole and buried.* Not like I have
a better idea. I don my official hard hat and orange vest
to unload my little shit into his truck. The hat slips
over my eyes and clunks off into mud.
Rain's really fucking us up, the man says.
He pulls on a bent cigarette.

I stare at the swelling sea of wet trash.
It feels like a stadium full of drunken fans
the moment it becomes clear that the game is lost.

Empty trucks turn around at the top
and file back down to make another run
like the giant black ants who tunneled
through my wet, rotted wood till I ripped it out.
The exterminator's coming tomorrow.

It cost me $57.86 to get rid of the wood. Minimum
charge for up to one ton. I could've brought at least
1000 more pounds at no extra cost. The exterminator
won't be cheap either. Maybe I should slip the ants $20
and see if they go away.

Back home, I pick out which ones to squish.
The biggest ones. They carry off their dead
to eat them. Last night a homeless man held out his cup
like he does each time I pass, and, as usual,
I gave him nothing.

Slip me a twenty, and I'll do a little
dance called the Exterminator.
Do you have any idea how many songs
have the word "babe" in them?
I thanked the man for the tip on future waste management.
He'll always have a job.

Reincarnation of the Peace Sign

In 1972, my father-in-law, painting the flashing
on his roof, asked his daughter arriving home from school
what he should paint on the chimney.

He escaped Yugoslavia in 1960 without the language
to tell his war stories. He had an inexplicable love
for Mohammed Ali, and nostalgia for simple bread.

You could drive by that house and never notice
the red peace sign, but once it's pointed out
you'll never miss it again.

He was always on a high ladder, trying to color
the miracle of his own home. So quiet up there,
he once told his daughter it was safe to cross

the street, then a bike ran her down, broke her leg.
The world always exacting its slice
of cruelty. How could he have forgotten?

In 2004, he gives me permission to repaint peace.
My legs tremble on the 30-foot ladder. I try to trace
his old lines, but make a mess of it. Beneath me,

my children shout my name. I can barely hear them
in the rarified air. If you drive by now—*peace*,
a little brighter, a little harder to make out.

If you drive by now, honk your horn and wave.
The old man's getting a little deaf. His English
as good as it's going to get. He's inarticulate

with rage at the war's daily news.
But if you raise two fingers into a V
he will nod, and nearly smile.

WINTER NOTION

I have this idea—imagine
a hawk sitting in the sun

in a bare December tree
and the woman jogging

past you on the city park trail
turning back to point at the hawk

so you won't miss it
and the hawk swooping low

over your head, raising hair
on your neck with the breath

of its long wings, and when she passes
you again, she asks *did you see it?*

and the sunlight catches her smile
and you stutter *yeah—yeah—*

it flew right over me. Red-tail.
Trail gently hugging the hillside,

the hawk embracing its silence.
No one to tell about it—the hawk,

the woman, the air swirling inside
like pagan grace, burning water,

red-tailed regret. Blow into your hands
for luck. See, that's my idea.

Rusty Jackknife

An address smudged off an envelope
half a phone number
the record stuck on a piano riff
the compulsion to list one's suicides
and one's lovers. How high
can you fly? How low can you go?

Faulty equations, unbalanced
accounts. Mislabeled occupations.
I've pushed the wobbly wagon down the aisle.
I mean road. I mean the cobble-stoned
time-line, the threaded needle stitching
off seconds, the attractive switchblade flick,
the swoop of one powerful arm
momentarily stopping discussion.

*

Switchblades are dated.
Last Friday one teenager shot another
across the street during an argument
no one seems to recall.

Fourth shooting in that three-story building
in fifteen years. I'm stumped
as to how bad that sounds. I don't have
any back-up singers. I call and get
no response. I wave and get
the finger back.

I haven't found anything quaint
in 183 days. I want somebody
to go down on me. It would mean a lot
to me. I would reciprocate.

*

My friend Paul Dilsaver
killed himself this summer
but I just got word today
because he used a silencer.
The size of antidepressants
is limited by the size
of the human mouth.

For example, who could swallow
a golf ball? Dilsaver published
pornography under his own name
and still tried to get a teaching job.
Twenty-two years ago, the poster
for his poetry reading showed him
jabbing a pistol against his temple.

That's what I call slo-mo.
A joke he might snort at.
He didn't have many friends left.
It's easier to call him friend now.

*

I'm going to slash a five
across the four sticks yet again
on the tiny paper graveyard on my lap.
I think I know who's next,

but I'm not telling. I'm not posting odds.
If I'm careful, I can clean my nails
with the blade, but who wants to be
careful today, the wagon flipping over,
the contents, whatever they might be,
frozen forever in the air.

ESPERANTOS

James Brown Esperanto
please, please, please

James Brown crying *please* 26 times.
Each time italics and boldface and underline
and superscript and hieroglyphics
and cave drawings and smoke signals.

The ache of your leaving/the missing
tooth of despair/the smashed headlights
of future fog rolling in/empty trellis/
sweet scent of miraged roses/torn
paper of bad erasure/stench of bus
grief/diesel sweat/burned cloth/guitar
string/strangulation/wrong tree cut down/
no putting it back/stump rotting
in its own sweet time despite 26 *pleases*.

Your face in the bus window, crumbling.
Out here, words on their knees.

Don Ho Esperanto
so here's to the golden moon

Tiny bubbles.
Tiny bubbles.
July acid trip.

Oozing snooze.
Country Western on Mars.
Twinkly champagne chatter.
Shatter safely on the dance floor.

Distant relative of a dead Irish uncle
known for his wedding medley.
Sing-a-long with syrup.
Sticky all over. Licky.

Crooner on the Mooner.
Leis and malaise.
Toes in tepid water.
Night life of mannequins.

JOAN JETT ESPERANTO
I don't give a damn about my bad reputation

audio hickey
lips unapologetic
electric wires dancing
like runaway fire hoses
and the flames doing
a little boogie they picked up
down the alley
faint whiff of the savory
unsavory knife whittled
to a voice tight as night
faint whiff of a drunken fight
angry gravel, angry unravel.

David Bowie Esperanto
cha-cha-cha-changes

A flash of metal trash in a vacant lot.
Mirage of glitter in the distance.
Sudden hiss of a punctured tire
on the edge of the universe.
Nobody to push the rest of the way
into free fall. Nobody but gravity.
The end of a beautiful nightmare.
What you would have sounded like
if she'd given you more time.
The churning robot soul sparking
with faulty wiring. The marriage
of a stilt and a crutch. Perfectly tuned
grind. Notes scribbled on the phrases
of the moon. The cynical faith
of the choir of sinners. A pout
and shout. Slippery when smug.
Bridge freezes before road. Cautionary
sneer. The heart pondering a change
of heart.

MILES DAVIS ESPERANTO
In a Silent Way

Ice breath night sky
pushing down subtle
yet unrelenting, letting
you know it's in charge.

Seconds have a way
of messing with you,
drilling their soft holes
till suddenly you've lost

your buoyancy
or your favorite hat.
Once, declarations were made.
Now, it's slur and popped

bubbles. Close your eyes
and imagine effortless
rowing. A world where money is liquid
and love grows on trees.

Tiptoeing with your bloody socks.
The moon's dissonance. A lingering
stranger's cry turned into a hymn
you're willing to pay for.

BESSIE SMITH ESPERANTO
gimme a pigfoot and a bottle of beer

Back of the paddy wagon
and where's that woman gonna sit down?

The piano as blunt instrument.
The saw cutting the woman in half.

Everything up her sleeve.
Even the sledgehammer weeps.

Every ice cube on the planet
melted in amber.

Broken-glass immunity.
Get-out-of-jail-almost-free card.

Let me unfold your fist
and hold your sweaty palm.

Let me kiss that little line
there.

AL GREEN ESPERANTO
love and happiness, yeah, something
that can make you do wrong, do right

below-the-belt interruption
delightful run in the stocking

not the first orgasm
the second or third

caught in a wave of silk hands

subtle electric aftershock hum

the word *love*
and each and every distant relative

trust of the growling dog
purr of the free-falling cat

moaning wetness
of the witness

lost in blurred erotic fog

gentle piercing
call and response

home on the ecstatic range
bass and treble stretched
into a fit

line busy
line off the hook

Jesus openly
appalled
secretly flattered

the days of the week
elided into one long midnight

the melting of clock hands
into bodily fluids

Sex Pistols Esperanto
no future for you

A rat burrowing into the corner
of the classroom, refusing
to accept the end of his punishment—
despite the teacher yanking on his arm.
He's fucking staying
in the fucking
corner.

Dog foaming at the mouth.
A man using that foam as shaving cream.
Teeth piercing skin. Repeat
as necessary. Learn to play
at your own peril. Leading the parade
into a cartoon version of hell.
The scratched lenses of rose-
colored glasses. The dripping spray
of aural graffiti. Artistic license
suspended. The soundtrack
of accidents, metal twisted
into balloon animals. Subsequently
popped. Subsequently used
as sex toys. Subsequently used
as fishing lures for rumored
undersea monsters. Subsequently
used as a new method for keeping
time. Subsequently used
as musical instruments.

LAURA NYRO ESPERANTO
come on, come on and surrey down to a stoned soul picnic

The swirled layered smoke dance
of the ancient tribe of the tragic heart.

The renaissance of the cowbell
and the downfall of Three-card Monte.

Late, out of breath for the planned break-up.
Nose running. Cold November. Sunny

with long shadows. A stranger's smile
on the empty street. Walking out

of the impenetrable lecture by the distinguished
idiot to find a bouncing ball chased by children.

The unapologetic intrusion of the soul.
God licking his lips. Her lips.

The secret shouted from a rooftop.
The echo shouting back.

The Abyssinian Baptist Gospel Choir Esperanto

let us say 'amen' again

Hammond B3 and an upright piano
duking it out, deep hum and thrum, anchor

of a bass beneath floating robes.
It's always Sunday morning in Esperanto-

land. Thick trees sway in whispered breeze
clapping out the code of transport

clickety-clack train melting the tracks
into the horizon, eternity

rising. Climb the ecstatic steps,
hold onto the thick exalted ropes

of song, and if you get there
if you arrive, say hello

in whatever tongue you're speaking.

Judy Garland Esperanto
from the moment I saw him, I fell

Fruity without the tutti.
A clown car full of ghosts.

Ice it, heat it.
Swelling and jelling.

Ooze and booze. Muscles
and bustles.

Blowing on the flames
till they're big enough

to dance on. Rooted
and booted. Fragile

and agile. Red meat.
A long time chewing

so you don't choke.

Marvin Gaye Esperanto

Marvin Gaye was shot by his father, April Fool's Day, 1984, one day short of his 44th birthday

Marvin startled his audiences in the early eighties when he shaved his head

Marvin onstage stroking the body of a spangled dancer
like a bearded, black Elvis on crank.

Marvin hip-shake smooth bump—no grind. Lipstick
on sweat. Marvin on Channel 9 from Windsor—

"Swingin' Time" with "Bobbin' Robin" Seymour—
lip-synching his way through white hell.

Marvin playing touch football with Berry Gordy
at Belle Isle in Detroit, believing he could make it

in the pros. Shirt off like a playground kid.
Shirt off, not thinking he's sexy. Thinking touchdown,

and a cool glass of water. Cool glass of water,
flames to the fire.

Lip-synching on "Swinging Time."
Shaving his head for the pain.

Marvin's halo tilted funky, tarnished
with bad love.

I'll trade Marvin sitting at the piano
dark stains under his long-sleeve shirt

for a Fat Elvis and two Johnny B. Goodes.
Marvin, I just want the long satin scarf

your tongue wove, the threaded grooves
of continuous play without the click

at the end, the crackle of fire, sizzle of grief,
the last imagined black moan.

Joe Cocker Esperanto
we've all forgotten we could fly

Bleeding is good for your
garden. Miracle cures occur
daily. Demons cast *in*.

Phantom limbs stitched
into dance. Somebody
might love you
if the wind's blowing right.

Full moon eclipsed
by the werewolf's hand puppets.

The accidental completion
of a wobbly circle.
The egg of a mythical beast.

Drastic measures
unmeasured. Crashing
the slurred party.

The beaten dog
returning for revenge.

The smoke
of the last smile
on the last train.

WARREN ZEVON ESPERANTO
I'll sleep when I'm dead

Asshole—somebody needs
to punch out the dude, wipe that smirk
off the jerk, but he's just gonna stagger
back to his feet and be a smart ass
all over again, doing that trick
where he swallows your sins.

LOU REED ESPERANTO
I don't know
just where I'm going

Heroin-stained sheets.
Frayed noose tickling.
Irony on holiday.
Bitterness embroidered.
Lead mainlined. Tasty grief
of survival. Awkward dance
of liberated marionettes.
Black gloves flexing strain.
Breath toxic with disappearance.
Dare and double dare
and so what. Showdown
slowdown. Wild horses
butchered on the streets
of New York. Shoulda known
better, coming in to the city
all frisky like that.

Frank Sinatra Esperanto
That's Life

Black baggage gleaming at the curb.
The melting knife trick. The lie
of memory. Expensive kisses
stolen and hocked. Life under
the table. Cutting in line. Getting
away with a shrug. Muscle behind
the muscle. Imaginary resort
where money is swallowed. Luck
and more luck. Cement-controlled sway.
Scripted tabloidathon. Secret sex
lives of the saints translated
by a blind pimp. Lock out
below. Lifting the false bottom.
Discretion of a shadow. Getting
what you paid for. Paying for
what you got.

DUANE ALLMAN ESPERANTO
Whipping Post with Dickie Betts

that guitar and another
in cosmic conversation
spilling reckless stars
words we cannot
birds we cannot name
the wheel of terror
at the joy pure
invisible indivisible
eyes shuttered
frenzy of notes
small watches
big time
whipping
slide
      post
slide
fossil of broken heart
centuries ago
hear me
centuries ago
thawed, revived
revised, testifying
to blindness
happy to be back
to tell the sad story
say it again
say it the same
say it different
get out while you can
get in while you can
the soul's coals smolder
a little bit of hell

for buoyancy
maps for kindling
two small matches
one big fire

Tiny Tim Esperanto
livin' in the sunlight, lovin' in the moonlight

The man at the door won't go away.
He wants *you* to sell *him* something.

Sticky knobs. Adjusting
seems necessary and impossible.

The choirmaster of cats waves his baton
and pokes himself in the eye: Oh!

Is everybody happity hoppity?
Giant by-jiminy clock hands. The faint odor

of turnips. God made a statement about clover
that was distorted by the press.

The toys of the world are mad
and aren't going to take it anymore.

They're forming an armed
choir of willing confessors.

You know how sometimes it's hard
to swallow, a lump of surreal madness

stuck back in there somewhere?
Like that.

Dusty Springfield Esperanto

the only one who could ever reach me
was the son of a preacher man

The voice in your sexual fantasies
of the last teacher you had a crush on.
The sound of that sweet spot, the hollow curve
down from the hip. The whispered
suggestion of fellatio. The shy smirk
and squint of daylight procedures.
Aftertaste of cotton candy and sperm.
The slip showing. The carefully applied
cover up. This little ache you're not telling
anyone about. Symphony of secret sweat.
The longest sigh, silk unwoven. Delicious shame.
Flashback to unguarded lust. Testifying
shout-out in a small, warm room. Antidote
to the confessional booth. Prosecutors grinding
their teeth at the elusive evaporation of proof.
Midnight, she skips naked around the block.
Or so it is rumored.

Tom Waits Esperanto

got me a chocolate Jesus
make me feel good inside

Vaseline and sandpaper

slow-mo saw, an eternal log

drooling dog on a rusty chain

cliché chafing skin

blind roar from a moist cave

toothy fish with a mouthful of hooks

the inability to accumulate material goods

and the generosity of your favorite fool.

Got a match? How about two? How

about a cigarette and a map, a good

tip on the meaning of life or a decent

racehorse? Batteries winding down

into the reincarnation of the hunch.

A shrug that ain't a shrug.

Herb Alpert and the Tijuana Brass

Esperanto

how can I show you
I'm glad I got to know you

Piling out of the clown cars
to be pallbearers at the funeral
of an unrelated lazy snake
who slithers out of the casket
and cooks breakfast for everyone.

Your grandmother being silly
dancing between cars in the hot parking lot
at the flea market where she will buy
ten useless objects
just to weigh her down a little.

Traffic jam translated into pedestrian.
A political meeting for dogs on strike.
Being polite to your girlfriend's hokey parents
when all you want to do. Well, everyone knows
what you want to do.

Bonnie Raitt Esperanto

yeah baby, I've been drinking,
and I shouldn't come by I know . . .

Who laughs loudest laughs proudest.
Who cackles, smackles.

Whiplash dynamite funneled
through a pinhole.

You gonna let that drunk chick kick
your ass?
                    She already did.

Bird dog boogieing on the high wire
above the imagination's dreamy net.

Dusty friends, and a big pot of something
burning. And, damn, it smells good.

Scrape the bottom of the pot.
All the good stuff stuck together.

A vague desire to start smoking again.
And taste a beery tongue just one more time

before the moon pulls its tiny string
to click off the light in the world's cozy closet.

Bobby Blue Bland Esperanto
I'll take care of you

You've got this drunk tiger
and this naked girl.
You've got these two guys
waiting for the police
outside their crashed cars.
You've got something taken outside
then back inside.
You've got this roller coaster
that killed somebody.
You've got this collection
you'd prefer not to talk about.
You're on the frequency
of horny dogs at midnight.
Don't adjust that dial.
Crush that dial. Eat
that dial. Memory ache
and something for the pain
just makes it worse.
The theory of magnification
versus the theory of magnetization.
The unfortunate lighting
of the fuse. Inconclusive
investigation of prayer. Vampire
blues exposed by the demolition crew.
The discarded theories of love
salvaged. Savaged. The missing
ingredient. The proximity. Predicting
the past. The smooth assurance
of the lost tour guide. Right this way.
You've got this drunk tiger
but he only wants to dance.

ELLA FITZGERALD ESPERANTO

the way you haunt my dreams, no, no,
they can't take that away from me

Sweet-gum smile. Moisture
in the folds. Flashbulb
smoke. Silk soiled
slightly.

The train full of all your friends
pulls into the station on time
for once.

Talking in tongues
as an Olympic sport.

Roller coaster laugh
and scream. The ride
that pays you when you get off.

Or tosses you out of your seat
into the stratosphere, depending.

The dignified meltdown
of the Tower of Babel
only to be reformed
into a choir of slightly naughty angels.

The Band Esperanto
Life is a Carnival

Popsicle melting on the ground
and hilarity all around. The horse
won't listen, but it's beautiful,
and the cat out of the bag
has its own bag with a dog
in it. A trail that narrows
into a hallucination. You know
you shouldn't, but you do.
Shake hands and come out
dancing. Wedding band
at the wake. The sinking ship's
annual cruise. Inland island.
The sun and the moon
unindicted co-conspirators.
Smoking on the porch. Cold
outside. Somebody's dead
but it's not you. One less person
to contradict your version of things,
and it's a damn shame.

THE TENURED GUY

THE TENURED GUY EXAMINES HIS CONSCIENCE

I once attended a meeting
about an ampersand
& I cast my vote for keeping it.

I dreamed I went to sleep
instead of attending the Raw Meat Festival.
I fell asleep kissing the feet of celebrities.

Watch out, I've been practicing
my bongos. From now on,
I'm going to end my poems

in the middle.
From now on, I'm going to lie
to my readers.

From now on, a wink and a nod
and a who-gives-a-shit.
This isn't really about

what you think it's about.
Is that post-modern
or pre-mature?

My real name is
Carl Yaztremski.
Yaz for short.

I've got 3000 hits
and 400 home runs.
I had my dick removed

and turned into a baseball bat.
Here, give it a few swings.

The sun's coming up.
Fastball outside corner.

Bless me father,
for I love closure.
Amen.

The Tenured Guy: Department Meeting, Friday Afternoon

Time to prepare for
the Review Committee visit.
Somebody sighs. Well, that means
another ad hoc committee.

The committee on committees
approves the formation
ad hocally.

Let's review the minutes
of last meeting. That comma
seems clearly, out of place.

You try not looking at your watch
for five minutes.

The Head—not a Chair
let's be clear about that!—
says from now on
Directors will be called
Coordinators.

Let's coordinate our watches:
fiiiiiive thiiiiiirty.
A yawn. A fart.

The Head invites everyone back
to the Main Office
for wine after the meeting.

A few laughs. A snort.
A few lower-case heads like yours
perk-up.

The Tenured Guy's Trajectory

The dean requests a narrative
of your goals for the next five years—
a new process called *post-tenure*
review. *Oxy-Moronic. New Formula—*

gets out stubborn stains. You want
to straighten the dusty framed
certificates on your office wall.
Not now—as a *goal.*

You accidentally made your way
into the recruiting brochure
checking out coeds on a warm spring day.
Is that a publication?

Trajectory: you draw a diagram
of the Texas Book Depository,
Oswald and Ruby together,
obscenely positioned.

Was that entirely necessary?
Your colleagues disparage you
as the holder of the endowed
Conspiracy Theorist Chair.

Can you list that as a field?
Cynicism wafts around you, stings
like a cloud of twenty-year-old
cigarette smoke. You could smoke

in your office back then.
And in the classroom. Outside, students
huddle, puffing in the cold. You wish
for an excuse to stand with them

that wouldn't kill you. The next
five years? Ten to retirement.
Your booster rockets fell harmlessly
into the sea years ago. No little form

is going to do the trick.
They're already bidding for the right
to press *eject* on your office chair—
talk about trajectory.

The Tenured Guy Calculates Salaries

You've got a formula
that figures in ass-kissing
and grade inflation. The pal
factor, the longevity factor,
the padded vitae factor,
the committee-wonk factor,
the self-promoting factor,
the gossip factor, the meeting-
attendance factor, the disagreeing-
with-the-head factor, the parking lot
factor and the cocktail factor,
the lame-publication factor, the rest room-
stink factor, the chewing-too-loud factor,
the jeans factor, the letter-to-the-editor factor,
the faction factor, the miniskirt factor,
the sports car factor, the too-chummy-with-student
factor, the not-chummy-enough factor, the dean-
and-provost-tennis-playing factor, the president's
son factor, the rich-alumni factor, the simple
royal pain-in-the-ass factor. Your raise: 2%.
You wander the hallways, poking into offices,
counting on your fingers. Adjusting
for the cost of living.

THE TENURED GUY GETS AMBUSHED

They surrounded him at the urinal
then tested his pee for impurities.
Whatever participles he possessed
dangled. They observed him washing
with syllabic soap and drying with old sonnets.
They tracked him down the hall and measured his feet.

He stroked the wood of the confessional. *And then
what did they do?* the priest prompted. *Nothing*,
he answered. *Sounds like the seminary*, the priest said.
The Tenured Guy then whispered a prayer
in praise of fucking and alcohol.

THE TENURED GUY TAKES HIS NEW HEAD TO THE BALL GAME

Two free tickets and no friends
so what the hell, ask the new guy.
Show him you know something
about some thing. He's an abstract
concept next to you, large belly wedged
into the tiny plastic chair out
in the cheap seats surrounded
by drunks from distant farmlands.
He claps politely when the sign says
CHEER! and LOUDER!
You sit on your hands, taking a stand
against the Jumbotron. He's critiquing
the hot dogs like an FDA inspector
waiting for a bribe.

3-2 top of the ninth. Cub runners
on first and second, one out. Line
drive to third-speared! Runner
doubled off. Game over!
You jump up, call him Petey
though his own mother probably
never did so. He's struggled up
out of his seat too. You try and give
each other high-fives, but keep
missing, two windmills
spinning toward the inability
to clarify an obscure point
at a future department meeting.

The Tenured Guy Learns to Cook

You were one of two tenured
among fifteen hired over ten years.
The old drunk who favored
young drama students but was too old
to grasp them in his tiny spider-like arms
patted your ass at parties. Harmless
enough, but he still had a vote. Once
while you were pissing at a urinal
he grabbed your neck and praised it
as *a wrestler's neck*. Harmless enough,
since someone walked in and he moved
away. He had a vote. Dinner invitations
you could not ignore, but always asked
to bring a date, a date bribed with cocaine.
She talked up such a storm, you snuck out
in the clouds and rain. You asked for his recipe
for whatever it was he made. He had a vote.
He complained when you grew a beard,
covered your *pretty face*. You shaved.
He had a vote and he gave it

to you. Years later, his drinking spills
into hallways, a coffee cup full of brandy,
his breath withering students in nearly empty
classrooms. He teeters
into incoherent monologues, his glasses
sliding off onto the floor with a clatter.
At the meeting to decide his fate,
you hold the index card with his mad scribble
350° for an hour and firmly state
we have to get rid of him.

He bitterly tosses his silver retirement cup
into a bag after the department has mustered
every good thing to say, every warm body
with a desire for free cake. A cut
on his forehead from a fall. You lick
the sweet frosting off your fingers
and step up to pray over the corpse.
You put your hand on his shoulder,
and he twitches.

THE TENURED GUY HANDLES THE EVIDENCE

In a class full of smooth faces
hers cracked into lines
like your own.

She's a sing-songy rhymer:
"Drunk Drivers Go To Jail."
God would get them

for killing innocents. *Don't preach*,
you told her. *My son*, she said,
was killed by a drunk driver.

That's truth. It's what I feel.
You gave her the standard advice:
Show don't Tell. Image over

Abstraction. She brings in
pictures of her son, and a pile
of his clothes—dumps them

on your desk with a drop slip.

THE TENURED GUY GOES INTO ORBIT

He lasted through graduation, a stick
in his heavy robe. Last time you saw him.
His poems about oral sex in the park

shocked the class. His easy laugh, his tilt
and lilt, won them over.
When he missed class, you thought it was

"senioritus"—till he returned
with his skeletal grin. Good poems.
Does it matter? Was he ever in love

before he died? You think of him today
as the Quilt passes through town.
He was just another kid experimenting

with dangerous chemicals. His poems said
I am alive and I am not afraid.
What planet is this, you wonder.

You'd like to make a rule that nothing
we do before we're thirty can kill us.
He won the "Newcomer's Award" that year,

a drama major come late to poetry.
If only he could have taken those poems back,
revised them into safety.

The planets seem safe in their distant orbits,
tiny balls of light, gentle, harmless,
like how you used to imagine it was here.

Was he lonely in that park, surrounded by darkness
and nameless stars? Brief couplings in cars, then
back into the cold, bearing saliva and semen

and not even a name. It isn't just that he was
the first you knew, or that he wrote well enough
to win a prize. It's not enough to say sex

should never kill anyone. But you say it anyway.
Making another rule. Another rule
for a planet you've sailed on past.

The Tenured Guy: Standards for Artistic Excellence

You've been putting off your standards statement
for weeks.

> Do penguins really smell that bad in Antarctica
> or is it just the zoo stench?

How's that statement coming? Your head asks
every time he sees you.

You've got tenure—you could propose anything.
You got through when they had no standards
statement. You put an acorn on your thumb:
*Hey Pierre, you with the snappy beret, what
kinda standards you got?*

The emeritus with fifty years in
sat next to you at the last meeting
doodling. His spirals had real
authority.

> They used to keep the gorilla in a cage
> with a tire on a chain for a swing—Bobo—
> he'd spit, and you'd run screaming.

How did we ever vote him through,
you imagine them thinking.

> *Hey Bobo,* you shout to the gorilla
> who's too far away, now living in
> his natural habitat. Animals don't have
> names any more.

And that's okay, you think
Standards change over time.

The Tenured Guy and the Chalk-throwing Incident

He was talking—disrupting class.
Again. You asked him to quiet down.
He kept on yapping.

You asked another student
to get his attention. *Hey*
and a tap, tap. No luck.

You lightly tossed the chalk.
It dropped on his shoulder,
fell to the floor. He stood,
demanded an explanation.

You told him if he couldn't be quiet
he should leave. He left,
said he was going to get you.
His thick finger stabbed the air.

Your head demanded an explanation
and formed a special faculty-
student committee to investigate.
The student made a chart
of the chalk's trajectory.
You'd never seen him so engaged.

The student newspaper said
you had to go. *Chalk Thrower*
scrawled on your office door
in ink. An apology was demanded,
and counseling.

Your colleagues shunned you.
Except for Jackson. Jackson, who sleeps
with his students whenever he can.
He put his arm around you.
Make love, not war, he said.

The Tenured Guy Reads His Student Evaluations

Scale of 1 to 5. His averages
scrawled in ink on a chart
in his locked cabinet
stuffed with faded blue dittos
blurred with ancient rage.

If he had his own baseball card
his statistics would resemble
those of a declining veteran
still on the roster, pinch-hitting,
mentoring the brash rookies,
hoping to hang on as a coach
or even some day a manager.

But he's full-time with ten years
until retirement and hates young profs
with their smarmy sneers and jeers,
moon-faced coeds trailing them down
the hall. His last swooner ended up
in Western Psych with vertical scars
and a chilling bone-glow through pale skin.

He used to clothespin baseball cards
to his bike spokes and imagine the power
of an engine. He jots down the latest
dipping scores. He drops a random file
into the trash without looking.

Those cards, if he'd saved them—
that girl, he wouldn't touch her—
the fine wine of bullshit
turning to vinegar.

The Tenured Guy on Sabbatical

In the country outside Paris, you begin
your research on texture and light
in the blah blah blah. You try to expand
your fictive breath into a novel.
You explore the nasal passages
of French poets. Whatever.

Your latest lover—whoever—paints
large black canvases in the studio
above you. Twenty years younger.
You gave her the better light.

The picturesque stones never get warm.
You spend mornings building fires
with wet wood. After a month,
you've got good technique and style—
your fires have style. You'll be sure
to include that in your final report.
Wet wood—an apt metaphor?

How will we get those canvases home?
you ask. You suspect she's along
for the ride. She'll drop you the minute
you're back on U.S. soil. She tromps
above you, mocking your silent keyboard.
Things are brewing, you tell her.
Good wine, and it's cheap.

A colleague FedExes to ask your help—
the department is hiring a new theorist:
write a letter supporting her
or else they'll hire somebody like that ass . . . .

Your colleague helped you a few years back
with that Thing-with-the-Student. *Hurry*,
she writes. Oh, sweet inspiration!
The words flow, effusive and generous:
Impressive credentials . . .
The ideal colleague . . .
Important doesn't begin . . . .

Feverishly, you work late into the night.
No dinner for me, you tell the painter,
I'm working!

Having a Little Talk with Capital P Poetry

When the dough-faced boy rhymed shellfish
and selfish in a preachy poem against smoking
at the open-mic at the hookah bar while I sat
fitfully on the floor on unplumped pillows
next to the only person in the room older than me
both of us stunned into various unrelated stupors,
when the reedy smirk of a girl in her fuck-me jeans
read about semen-stained sheets and giggled
every time she said fuck, when the angry
math major squealed his brakes at the end
of every line to make sure we caught his
thine pine wine sign O woe is him,
when the harsh hostess berated us
into continuing our applause to drown out
the hookahy background music,
I just wanted to pop the balloon of their Big P
and give them a hug that hurt and pull them
down below the lower-case p with the worms
and dirt and rocks and spit. I wanted
to give self-expression a bad name, or an alias,
or a mustache of dirt like the little boy
who's been quietly eating it alone
and at peace in some small corner
of what we might all agree
is the world.

Biting Off More

than hunger calls for
than your teeth really want
      to spend time with
than your tongue feels
      righteous about
than your share
than the metric equivalent
than a fistful of dollar bills
than

NEVER IN MY WILDEST DREAMS

all dreams are wild—
ever try to fit a pair of pants
      onto a dream?
And that's just the ones
      you remember.
What about all those other
      swampy things
disappearing into the murk,
      just a few bubbles rising
off the surface?
              Maybe it should be
never in my most *selfish success-driven* dreams.

The camera's zooming in on the big fake smile
while down below nobody's wearing pants—
never in my wildest genitals!

MAKING A MOUNTAIN OUT OF A MOLEHILL

is the poet's job.

SWINGING FOR THE FENCES

for the next vine
conveniently spaced

then one day there's no vine

and you can move the fences in
and still call them home runs

I suppose. Or you can take an
intentional pass

or pull out the tarp and cover the infield
and call the game due to anxiety.

Oh the glory of the swinging strike
the quiet whish, the quiet wish
disappearing

because we are human
because we want change for a twenty
because we still lick the photographs
of old lovers and sharpen popsicle sticks
into daggers and

MAYBE IT'S JUST ME BUT

in the free-for-all
free fall
it's hard to tell
if everybody's waving goodbye
or grabbing at the air
for someone to hold onto.

Attendance Police

A student called to say that halfway to class
she got sick and turned around. Chemo,
and mornings are the worst. 19, worried
about her grade—something that can
be changed. I keep forgetting she might die.
Talk more in class, I say.

Okay, you try it.
Try to say something reasonable.

*

Last week, another student cried
when she couldn't get her work in on time.
She fell apart in the hallway
while I shielded myself with books.

I said with some confidence
that it'd get better. She needed sleep
and maybe a new boyfriend, though I tried
to keep her from going there.

*

My son and I got haircuts together last week.
He got a buzz job. I got a semi-buzz. Old-guy
buzz. Leave me something to yank at.

My white hair and his brown sailing down
on top of each other, easy as a dream
that makes you want to go right back
to sleep because nothing in the waking world
makes you that calm.

*

She's losing her hair.
Her boyfriend shaved his in solidarity
though he's one of those hunks
who makes no hair look pure and natural.

He meets her after class
to see how she'd holding up/in/out/steady.
His face, talk about scared.

*

9:00 a.m. and we're talking fiction
Mondays and Wednesdays. She's talking
more, suddenly into things that are both real
and not. Eighty minutes when it's not her life
everybody's thinking about.

*

The crying girl talks a lot too.
She's heavy and sad and her name
is Catherine. The other girl is Emma.

They sit on opposite sides of the room.
They're talking too much
about what characters they like and don't like.

We're supposed to be talking about
dialogue and point of view and flashbacks
and flash forwards and flash in the pans.

*

On the syllabus I typed Attendance Police
instead of Policy. I got a few jokes out of that
but they're expired now.

I have three kids named Timmy in the class.
What are the odds of that? And nobody
wants to be called Tim, go figure.

One's name is Timmy Newcomer.
I wish I could be a newcomer my whole life.

He names all his characters Mitch
and Zoey. And there he goes babbling on
till I'm convinced he hasn't even
read the story we're talking about.
Timmy, just *listen*, I'd like to shout.

*

Hair on the barber shop floor.
My son still holds my hand once
in a while. He gets mad when I say
I'm old. Maybe we should all
get our hair chopped off.

Emma's *life*
is too short.

DEFEAT IN THE CITY GAME

Hammering

In my grandfather's low cellar in Detroit
you had to duck constantly in the dim light.
A vise sat on each end of his workbench.

Always a reason to put something in
and squeeze tight against disappearance.
A chunk of wood, whatever.

He lost a boy in high school, a boy just when
he wasn't a boy anymore. A boy then, forever.
On the workbench, two dented meat loaf pans,

one for nuts, the other, bolts. I'd run my hands
through them like gold. But nothing shone brightly.
Nothing rusted. They were coated with oil,

not abandonment, nor grief entirely.
Each muffled clink of metal against metal
a small compromise or promise or lie.

Some of those nuts matched some of those bolts
kept apart to match orphans outside the pans.
To replace the loosened and lost. I could've gone

blind down there, but he'd learned to lean into
the dark, to tighten every single thing another turn.

He lost a daughter too. She *was never right.*
Imagine the day they figured that
out. A baby forever. Or until age twelve

when she matured into death. Who am I
in this story? The boy hammering nails into wood
and calling it a boat. A pile of coal sat in the corner

black against itself, unlit forever, the furnace
converted to gas. Black dust, the one thing rising.
I loved the mystery of coal and my grandfather's

odd, squeaky voice. His company, Packard, went belly
up and took his pension with it. Didn't leave much
for a new washer. Didn't leave enough to get him

the hell out of there, houses burning down around him,
or worse, filling with crack vials. I see I missed a third line
back there. That's how fast it happened. Lucky he'd

practiced the stoop all his life. Luck rattling in those
meat loaf pans like a beggar with a cup of pennies.
I knew some of them matched, and some didn't,

but down in the dark, I learned it over and over again.

Tonight a Reckless Cyclist

swerved a left turn
into my headlights as I drove
        through the intersection,
my teenaged son beside me complaining
        about being my teenaged son.
I smashed my foot against the brake
        and the tires shrieked and my heart
and my son's heart shrieked the silent shock
        on the cyclist's face
as he braked rather than sped
        and I swerved around him.

Nice going, dad, he said as I coasted
        downhill. *You ran that light.*

It was yellow. He wasn't wearing
a helmet, had no light on his bike,
what's he doing driving at night
like that, going to get himself
killed.
        My son makes this noise
he picked up from his friends,
a mannered hiss designed for maximum
parental rage.

I know I shifted tenses. *Makes,*
continues to make. I wear a hat he hates.

I was picking him up from rehearsal
for a play he was begging me not to see.
In the front door, and he's gleeful:
Dad almost killed some guy
He ran a red light.

You start out with a neat structure and end up
swerving into chaos, the road disappearing
into underbrush, the wide, groomed trail
narrowing to a fine line.

Yellow, I said. *Yellow light.*
We used to play Red Light/Green Light.
I used my arms as barriers. He loved when I pulled him
into the jail of my lap for ignoring the signals,
trying to swerve past my extended arms.
I'm ignoring some signals now, I'm sure
some parenting book would tell me.

The lesson is. The moral is. The correct response
        is. None and all of the above.
Impossible to cheat. No answer key,
        no ultimate authority.
I almost killed a kid tonight. I can hear the crunch
        of a bike mangling beneath my tires.
My wife and daughter are silent in their own
        landscape of electric wires and hidden panels.
I wear my magician's hat. What's for dinner?
        How about a bowl of lead paint chips?

I made the house safe for them so that they can leave
        the house and become unsafe. What's
the biker doing now? Are his hands atremble
        as he attaches his kryptonite lock?
Safety first, love second, grief third, anger
        rounding the corner for the head-
first slide.

He doesn't want me to see the play.
        The light was pink. The trees were stoic.
The sidewalk bland with cracks. Red light.
        Green light. He's gone up the stairs.
My daughter slides past to follow.
        My wife asks *is he alright?*
I don't know, I say, *I don't know.*
He didn't have a light, I say.
Everybody has a light, she does not say.
I'll keep trying to find it, I don't say.

That's a dark street, she says.

Tarnish

For homework, my children have to find
a penny from each year of their lives, then
write one sentence for that year. Eight and nine,
son and daughter, weedy hair sprouting wild.

We water it down, comb it neat,
but it springs up unruly.

*

1962. At the Holy Name Society picnic
the men buried pennies in a pit
and let us go at it. Fistfuls of sawdust
and copper. Paper-cup ice cream
and multi-colored pop, the holy name
of greed—who could swallow the most?
Six pops, the record.
It wasn't mine.

*

I can barely read the dates
as my thumb flattens Lincoln's hair.
We line them up, a record
of tarnishing. How many years does
it take, on average? One sentence
per year? One word? One letter?
Heads or tails?

*

My record was three, pissing it away
in the fly-ridden outhouse,
pocket sag of pennies and the priest's
drunken grin behind me.

In the sawdust pit, somebody pried away
what was mine. I shoved aside my little brother—
mine, mine, mine. We were mining
the beginning of the rest of our lives.

I don't know the year, but that's
my sentence.

Wildflowers Dying in a Cracked Vase

We bought a cottage from an old woman named Babes
who questioned our separate last names.
Young, imagining life endless and unbandaged,

a son and daughter of the working class, stepping
up from our parents' basement rec room.
We bought a cottage on a small nameless pond

referred to as "the lake" by locals who ate the fish
and swam, oblivious to farm runoff, as we were, at first,
young, imagining life endless and unbandaged.

We pumped poisons in to try to keep bugs, critters,
algae, and locals at bay. Our parents were dying.
We bought a cottage on a small nameless pond

but sold it to Bruno, a numbers man who owned a boat
too big for that pond. Our rubber raft sank.
Young, imagining life endless and unbandaged,

we bargained poorly to return to the clutter and clang
of city lives. We welcomed back our wounded dollars.
We sold our cottage on a small nameless pond.
Young, imagining life endless. Unbandaged.

THE GARDEN STATE

My children drop paper clips into dirt
to mark their tomato and pepper plants
in our tiny garden. I'd said *popsicle sticks*,
but they translated. My wife called the neighbor
to the fence in the quiet of morning hoses
to ask her to go inside for their future fights.
Our children cannot translate their hard words
into something harmless. My daughter's
pet slug died. She gave it a proper burial.
Others eat my lettuce. After rain, the paper clips
shine. It's been quiet next door for days.
Soon, they will rust. The wife might lose custody
of her son to her married daughter. I offer to cut
our roses bending over their side of the fence.
She wants to build a trestle instead to take
advantage of our growth. 302 miles away,
my parents are packing up their home of 43 years
to move into a condo. Her kid, a sullen
skateboard punk. His stepfather has two kids
from another marriage and no special affection
for him—that's a translation of what we've heard.
The rose bush is at least ten feet high.
My daughter's set up a chair under our trestle
and calls it New Jersey. The bush grew
from a cutting taken from my parents' house
in Warren, taken from my grandmother's house
in Detroit, taken from her great grandfather's farm
in Bay City. The smell is sentimental and sweet.
The fights are bitter, the acrid smells of gunpowder
and grief. The paper clips will get buried beneath green
till we can identify nothing. She said they'll fight
in the basement from now on. We'll see.
We'll listen as the petals fall.

Walking My Son Home from Preschool
St. Julien de Peyrolas, France

From the hilltop village we circle
down through dust, disappearing
into grapevines just budding
green through gnarled wood.

I hold his hand stumble-bumble.
We edge to the roadside for the nearly
imaginary cars, mirages
of dust wisps and tire-crunch.

We pick wildflowers looping along ledges,
edges. We are tiny shoots ourselves,
back and forth across the road,
connecting delicate colors.

The French he's heard all morning
buried in the odd corner of his brain
reserved for animal sounds. We can hear
a horse miles away, clearing its throat.

The world refuses to be uppercase
under the perfect noon sun, the huge blue
cloudless parentheses. We are random
commas heading home, refusing to subordinate.

Our flesh hums through each other's fingers.
We don't worry about French words
for this or that. Or English words,
or words in general.

Defeat in the City Game

We stood waiting for the school bus
while three men argued over a stolen
cell phone. Me, my son, my daughter.
7: 53. Where's the damn bus?
The big guy jiggling his hammy fist
vs. the little guy with baggy pants,
the ragged splinter of a junkie wedged
between them. Baggy pants, hand
in his pocket, claimed he had a gun,
gonna blow the hammy head
off. We're just a cute little family
of statues in the line of fire. Hammy
charged off around the corner,
the bus came, my children climbed on,
the other men vanished.

And there it is. Elusive It, fugitive It.
Scary It. Irrational—or just practical—It.
Back home with my rolodex
of potential actions I could/should
have taken, I slashed around
what/whether to tell my wife,
what my children were actually
aware of. I promised to stop using
the word *actually* so much.
It's losing meaning in terms
of what was in baggy's pocket
though he claimed it was
loaded. Next day, I told the driver
we're waiting across the street
from now on.

As the last seconds ticked off
and my children's hands turned to ice,
as the crowd filed out of the arena,
as the clouds drifted by unnoticed.
It. 7:53. The zeroes
of my children's eyes
narrowing.

DREAM WITH A TRAIN IN IT
after Edwin Reyes

Considering the lack of oversight,
the lack of tracks, considering
the shunned moon and the bitter
grit of stars, the bed's gravelly silence
and the idling tinted-window
bass-thump SUV, the melting ticket
and the grim cyclops conductor,
it was pleasant to waken, my son waving,
rattling the sports section in front of me
like a panicked sailor to read me some score,
the pages drifting apart and down
to the dusty floor of our tiny station.

THE NAME OF THE PLACE

I am trying to remember the name
of the place Jim's band used to play at
over on Van Dyke and the name of the place
on the edge of town we went Sundays
when our regular place was closed
and the name of the place on Mound
where we played pool and the other place on Mound
that let me keep a tab and the place on Schoener
with free popcorn and the place on Dequindre
with the country band, but too many bars
have shuffled past, stomped and soft-toed past,
slid and spun past.

The place where Marcy and I hugged and cried
when we ran into each other years after
my divorce from her sister, the topless place
I ended up at the week before my wedding
where I ate a cherry off a dancer's breast
as if it were a vitamin to take away my sadness,
the after-hours place down on Woodward
where I got my ass kicked I don't quite
remember why, the place down by the river
with the hot blues bands and resident drug dealer.

I have sat here for hours, there for days, months,
but the names are gone, pissed away like the names
of women I slept with. Some days I want to remember
the names so bad, as if remembering might be enough
to prove the time was not wasted.

You might go in some of these places
and shove my photograph under a bartender's nose
like a tough cop. He might say *yeah* or shake his head.

He might laugh and nod, or curse and nod.
I could show you places I got kissed and/or beat up,
the gravel I fell onto in rutted parking lots.

If I let this fistful of gravel slide out
between my fingers, it will fall to the ground.
When you walk out at closing time
all bars are the same.

If there is a moon, it will be a silent moon.
And whether you are alone or with a lover
or with a good friend or two, you will *feel* alone
with all the clean cold air surrounding you.
You will start your car, turn on your radio.

In the morning, you will not remember
what you listened to. You might remember
turning up the radio, but you will not remember
the song. You will try to remember
a joke someone told you, something that seemed
funny, or try to remember an idea you had,
one that would make money or mend your heart.
You will remember your own name
and be anxious, eager, to trade that name
for a punch line, an offhand remark,
for a song, just the name of a song.

Bag of Clothes

The hospital gave my father a bag
containing the clothes they cut off
my brother so they could get to him—
wire him up, sew him up, pump him up
full of air air air.

We're driving to, or maybe home
from the hospital, the hour and a half
each way to Saginaw past Crappo St.,
and that joke got old days ago

and my father says
out of the thick hospital silence
that clouds us everywhere
they gave me
his leather vest and jeans

the words hang like—
my father keeps adjusting
the air conditioning and blowers—
he's driving or I'm driving
we take turns and he says
after letting it hang, dangle, droop
says *I threw them out.*

My brother's alive. Slashing
at the underbrush with his machete
to rejoin us here in the world.
We rejoice over his first word—
bathroom—like first-time parents:

he said *bathroom*
did you hear him say *bathroom*?
I heard him say *bathroom*.

I think my father wanted me to say
something about the clothes. To see if I knew
some protocol for their disposition. His son,
my brother, age 53.

My father doesn't like to run the air—
it cuts down on mileage. He turns it
off, he turns it on.

It's hot. *Leave it on.* But I say
nothing. My father can't stop talking
to the son who understands him.

We both want my brother to return from his trip
without souvenirs or foreign currency.

Bloody clothes. Naked body slapped
on the slab, a frenzied swarm
trying to save him.

Did he put the bag inside another
bag? Did he take it out with the trash?
Or did he drop it in a green barrel
at rest area #1 or #2 between Detroit
and Saginaw?

I'm guessing the barrel option
and some weird guilt giving him
hot or cold flashes. I'm guessing,
and we're talking about what?
Not Crappo St. again.

We've never ridden in a helicopter.
Steam rises off the road after the briefest
of rains. No respite. *If it would only just
rain*, he says. The rending of garments.

The reliance on medical personnel.
Do we have enough gas to get home?

He plays some strange mix tape
my brother gave him that combines
country music with the Irish Tenors.
The vest. The jeans. It loops endlessly
till one of us shuts it off.

The Wrist

I saved the tiny hospital I.D. bracelets cut
from the luminous wrists of my newborn children.

In the yard, my son smashes black-eyed Susans
with his errant free throws.

As an experiment, my daughter planted a sunflower
seed on the window sill.

The wrist's bare skin. A little moist where it
meets the hand, two small stitched lines of skin.

My old best friend has stopped answering mail
since his daughter died. I cannot lick his stamps.

My father misses his tomato plants. My mother
misses her rose bush. Spring, and they are moving.

Have moved. Continue to move. Here, sunflowers
rise from the dirt like my children.

My daughter thinks I've shortened
her playground slide. My son suddenly sinks

a long shot from the tree stump. The black-eyed Susans
come back every year. My rose bush blossomed

from a cutting from my mother's. The ball rolls
down the driveway into traffic. So far, only I

am allowed to retrieve it. I prop up the smashed stems.
It's all in the wrist, I tell him. *Shoot like waving goodbye.*

Indecipherable Elegy

Three dreams and one blurry whisper.
Awake, I remember your last name. The moon

could be twisting itself into your wind-blown hair
behind those clouds. I wait for the last track

but Miles has put his trumpet away
in the dark room and disappeared like you.

A leaky drum of rain silently decoded
by ancient animals left out in it.

The ghost of your face emerging
on a smudged sheet of erasures.

A red leaf curling toward brown.
I awoke with an electric heartbeat.

Power returns with the clock's flashing
numbers. To be reset by faith.

Hammering

This morning after breakfast
my daughter asks to borrow a hammer
in the voice of a busy carpenter
or a wizard in search of a wand.

My *what for* goes vaguely unanswered,
my shrug taken as *yes*. She grabs it
from the toolbox, her thin arm yanked
down by the weight.

She pulls leaves off bushes
and on the stump of our old cherry tree
she hammers them on a piece of paper
according to a system established
by ancient astronomers
or insane mathematicians.

Later I find the paper on my desk
patterned with lush powdered green.
Tomorrow she may invent the wheel.
Today I gently rub the dust of my bones.